Stories From A Couple Idle Minds
Stories That Spark Your Imagination
Vol 1

Kevin Pamon & Erica Johnson

Illustrated by Edward Johnson Jr and Anniyah Pamon

Edited by Jamila Gomez

DEDICATION

This book is dedicated to our loving mother Janice M. Pamon who passed away in 2006 and friend Kenyon T. Simmons who passed away in 1998.

Table of Contents

ACKNOWLEDGMENTS

We would like to thank God for humor and we would like to
thank all our family and friends for their support.

Section I.

The Art of Storytelling

Stories From A Couple Idle Minds

Young Visionary Converses with Big Sister

Little Brother, who is a genius and advanced in his thinking by many years, sits down to converse with his sister. He is a very humorous person but many people do not find him funny. He does not have many friends and the only one who understands him, or should I say entertains his conversation, is his big sister.

Little Brother explains, "Did I tell you about the time I saw a mountain fish galloping along a trail?"

Big Sister chuckled, "A mountain fish…galloping? Something tells me that you will be able to express your vision in the most distinct fashion, as to give me a dynamic picture of the fish as you saw it."

"I must say this was the happiest fish I had ever seen in my life," Little Brother continued. "He had so much grace in his gallop. With each leap he would flick his fin twice and the sunrays bounced off of its scales. I tried to run after the fish and wanted to capture it to keep it as my pet. As I headed for the fish, his stride became faster and he vanished. I was upset that I could not catch the fish and found myself lost in the wilderness. Then I heard a twig snap. I looked to my side and there was the fish, sticking his tongue out at me. Then he said, "Meow"."

"AHHHH!" Big Sister exclaims with laughter. As I expected, you have once again catapulted my laughter into uncontrollable choking! I sit and ponder how you are able to think with such intensity, such passion and such luster. Then, it flanks my mind that you have a special something that has caused this to perspire from you. I think back and attribute your creativity to the time when you swallowed the yak cheese."

Little Brother is thrown back. The thought of making cheese from a yak's milk was ingenious. Little

5

Brother was encouraged by his big sister's words and creativity. Then he decides to go right into another story!

"I was walking in the jungle and I saw a lion. He looked so sad as he walked with his head down. I never saw a lion with such a low self-esteem. I said to him, "Keep your head up. Things will get better". Then I noticed he had the neck of an ostrich!"

His sister shows that she has been given this same "superpower" of storytelling as her younger brother. Little Brother thought he was the master of storytelling, but she leaves her brother astonished with her closing remarks.

"I am sorry, but this one leaves me a bit dazed and confused. Now, correct me if I am wrong, but why were you walking in the jungle? I though you knew that everyone surfs in the jungle!"

They leave quietly, chuckling to themselves in amusement, thinking about the possibilities of a galloping fish, a lion with the ostrich neck, and actually eating some yak cheese. They really amused themselves with thinking of possible flavors of this cheese.

Today is a Good Day Part I

Little Brother tells his sister, named Big Sister, about his day. Little Brother lives in the basement of his parents' house in Chicago. In the basement, there is not much heat. Every morning Little Brother walks across the cold basement floor to go upstairs to take a shower. Sometimes he looks out the window to see the sun shining, but the air outside is freezing cold.

"I walk upstairs and looked out the window and the sun was shining. *Today is a good day,* I thought to myself. I opened the door and took a deep breath and my tongue froze," Little Brother explained to Big sister.

The washroom is in the back of the house across from his parents' room. Catty-corner to his parents' room there is another bedroom, in which his little sister is asleep.

"I got in the shower and allowed the warm water to run down my head," Little Brother explains with fluid hand gestures and reminiscent facial expressions. "It felt like a massage going from my head to my back. This was wonderful! All of a sudden, the warm water turned into a hard blast of cold water that made my toes crack. I was in a state of shock and quickly fumbled to turn the water off. I scurried out of the shower and there were no clean drying towels available. The only available towel I see hanging from the towel rack was a dried up face towel. You could see that this towel was stiff from previous use. This was a towel that I used yesterday to clean my armpits. I had two choices: run across the cold floor in the basement where my bedroom was or dry off with the sour face towel. I am glad for choices in life. They keep things exciting."

"What happened, what did you decide?" asked Big Sister in anticipation.

"I decided to make a mad dash for my room. So I ran past Mom and Dad's room in the hope that no one would see me running down the hallway naked. I ran down the stairs to the basement and came to the realization that all the lights were out."

Big Sister is chuckling heartily as Little Brother tells the story. Big Sister knows about the house and the basement. In the basement there are a few windows, but they have thick blinds through which no light can enter. There is also one bedroom and an old washer and dryer. Oftentimes, clean clothes and towels are folded on a table in the basement.

Little Brother continued, "After taking five steps in the darkness, I began walking very slow because I did not want to trip and fall. This is great! I am wet, cold, and walking slow. When I am halfway to the table where the clean clothes are, I find one of my toys that I have not seen for about 10 years under my foot. The toy happened to be a car. One foot decided to ride the car and the other foot stayed planted on the cold floor. My foot rode the car until my bones did not want to stretch anymore. I ended up laying on the cold basement floor, in the dark, with no clothes on, and wet."

"Then I heard a click at the top of the stairs leading to the basement. Someone turned on the light. The last thing I wanted was for anyone to see me on the floor naked. I looked up, and to my amazement, it was just my pet fish bringing me my bath towel. I love that fish!"

Big Sister laughs at how her brother ended his true story with a little fiction. As usual, Big Sister goes along with the story and even gives the fish a name.

"That is beautiful!" says Big Sister. "I'm astonished at all of the things you can be grateful for before you even leave your house. How old is Lester the fish now? His name is Lester, right?" Big Sister continues. "He hates it when I get his name wrong. My morning was less eventful as yours, but I too have a lot to be grateful for nonetheless.

Today is a Good Day Part II

Big Sister was always glad that Little Brother shared his walks on the wild side with her, and she in turn shared her wacky stories with him. "Today is a good day, I agree," Big Sister says. "I got up to study and read a bit, only to find that my 4-year-old daughter, Faye, wanted to read from my book the night before. Unbeknownst to her and me, she accidentally misplaced it. Most mornings I would not mind looking for it, as we do share most items in the house, but this morning I had arisen slightly later than normal, which cut into my reading time."

Big Sister did not go and ask Faye where she put it, for she was told earlier, "I am young and I need my rest. Therefore, if you see me resting, do not awaken me, although I have the liberty to do this to you. Do you understand?"

"I would have to be a fool to tell her 'no', so I passively just nodded in agreement. As I looked for my book, I noticed that there were a lot of dirty cups lying around from my other children, so I commenced to pick them up. As I was doing so, my eye caught an old crusty potato chip on the floor, so I went to get the vacuum. Before I could look for the vacuum, I thought it wise to use the bathroom. On my way to the bathroom, I saw there was only a little bit of tissue left on the roll, so I scurried carefully up the stairs to go into the closet for more. I glanced down at my watch on my way up the stairs and realized that I was supposed to wake Tiara, my 17-year-old daughter. I thought, *I got to get her out of bed and get her ready for school*." Big Sister had to do this without waking Faye. The rule was already given to her.

"I startled Tiara as I awoke her and she, in turn, woke my 6-year-old son, DC. He said he wanted milk, so I went back downstairs to pour him some milk."

"Why did I go upstairs, anyway? 'God is good,' I softly mumbled to myself. But since it was not brought back to my remembrance, I continued down the stairs. I looked through the front window as I went down the stairs and saw that the garbage man was coming and we had not set our garbage out. Without any hesitation, I darted into the garage, raised the garage door, then yanked the cans out and ran down the long driveway. On the way out the garage I wondered if I had awaken my 12 year old daughter, Marissa. Oh well.. Halfway down the driveway I felt kind of cool. When looking down, I noticed where all of the air was coming from. To my embarrassment, there I stood, unpresentable, and very vulnerable for all to see. I made a mad dash back into the garage, dragging the teetering cans behind me. As I ran into the house, I headed straight to the bathroom, tripping over the vacuum, and sat in shock at what had just transpired. Lifting my head, I noticed that the book I had been looking for was lying on the floor between the toilet and sink. Geez, will anything get done?"

"My goal for tomorrow: Do more, by doing less."

The Bus Ride

Little Brother tells his Big Sister about his ride home on the bus. Little Brother goes to work every morning with his father. They work at the same company and they drive to the train station where there is a bus that is designated for employees at their company. This bus only makes about four stops and the ride can be anywhere from an hour and forty-five minutes to two hours and forty-five minutes, depending on the traffic. The majority of the people on this bus get off at the first stop and only four people get off at the last stop, including Little Brother.

"Yesterday it rained, which caused my bus ride to be long. After sleeping for about an hour and a half, usually my bus is close to my stop. As usual, I didn't open my eyes until the last couple of minutes of the ride," says Little Brother. "I figured that the only people left on the bus were the regulars; two ladies and Dad."

Little Brother grabs his stomach and makes a distinct face, "I had been holding in some air from lunch (beans and rice), and felt it was a good time to relieve myself. So, I did a slight body shift and allowed a nice smooth gust of air to exit and tried to continue sleeping. After riding for about ten more minutes, I started to get uncomfortable and wondered what was taking so long for the bus to get to our stop."

Big Sister, with a look of bewilderment, says, "No you didn't!"

"I opened my eyes and noticed that we had not even made it to the first stop. The bus was still full. Some people were sleep but there were others that were wide awake. I did not dare to give anyone eye contact at that moment. I don't know what the people thought of me afterwards."

Poetry Showdown

Little Brother understood that Big Sister could tell a story just as well as he. Little Brother decides to change the subject and throws some poetry at his sister to see how she would react.

"I call this "Left with a Kiss"," said Little Brother.

"I was in love and she kissed me.
I did not want to wash my face.
I often thought about her large beautiful lips.
I had been mesmerized until it started to itch. Then a rash appeared.
But now I notice her lips were swollen.
That was not lip-gloss that she wore, but rather ointment."

Little Brother finishes with his chest sticking out and a smile on his face and says, "What you got?"

Quickly Big Sister says, "I call this "Togetherness"."

"Like white on rice, that's togetherness.
Like stink on a skunk, that's togetherness.
Like fuzz on teeth after a good nights rest, that's togetherness.
Like glue on dentures, that's togetherness.

Like the fart of a loved one that lingers, that is togetherness.

Like the sock on your foot that has been worn all day inside of your hot boot, that's togetherness.

When it is all said and done, togetherness is what keeps us one."

As soon as Big Sister finishes, Little Brother speaks in a bold manner, "Days of Courting!"

"I look into your eyes and notice a fish swimming.

We walk together on a beach barefoot and I step on some broken glass.

You whisper sweet nothings in my ear and leave me with a moist ear.

We go into the wilderness and gaze at the stars, and then a bird flies over us and drops something white in your eye.

After we kissed on the first date, I noticed the smell of chitterlings lingering in the air."

As Big Sister opens her mouth to speak, Little Brother yells, "I Sing".

"I sing because I am happy.
I sing because I am free.
I sing because Jordan finds it funny.
I sing to see what notes I can produce for the day.
I sing because my throat is itching for a scratch."

"I sing too," says Big Sister.

"I sing because I'm happy.
I sing to make the dogs howl.
I sing because it sounds unlike music to others ears.
I sing because it's free."

"Before you cut me off like before, I call this "Close of the Day"," says Big Sister.

"A few things can be said to be absolute, but there is always an exception.
I can say that I absolutely hate flying, except if you push me off a cliff.
I can say that I absolutely don't like to exercise, except if you offer me enough money.
I can say that I absolutely love cars, except the one that ran me over.
But one thing I can say, this is absolute without and exception…
When 5:00 hits, that is absolutely the close of the workday!"

Portrait of Little Brother

Portrait of Big Sister

Squirrelly

Big Sister, always being unpredictable quickly fires back with a parable to show Little Brother that she is the master in the art of storytelling.

We grew up together but never really noticed how different we actually were. He seemed to always have energy and tended to gnaw at his food. I questioned why he couldn't eat what the rest of us ate. Upon his 17th birthday, I quickly put a little surprise in his food. One would think, having been around him for a long time, I would know what he liked. As we celebrated, he became a little different. I could not put my finger on it, but Squirrelly was not quite so squirrelly. As he combed his thick hair, I noticed that there was more on the floor than on his back. *Was the surprise I gave him having a negative affect? Don't they eat foods like us? I guess not.* Not to alarm Squirrelly, during the night, I silently glued the patches back on. Since Squirrelly had no sense, this went on for a while until I noticed that he did not comb anymore.

I asked Squirrelly, "Why don't you comb your hair anymore?"

He replied, "I have been trying to shed my fur to get a new layer, and somehow I keep getting old hair."

I figured I didn't know Squirrelly as well as I thought, for the surprise had backfired. He did not need glue. What he needed were hair clippers.

So, the next night, I hopped on to the idea to use Nair hair remover, because I had no clippers in the house, to help him achieve his goal of getting his new fur. Excited about what I had done during his sleep, I awoke with a jolt, anticipating his reaction to his new hairdo. Thinking he would be as excited as I was, I hurried him to a mirror as soon as he awoke. How was I to know that he could have heart attacks as we do? I will never know whether or not he liked his new hairdo, for that morning, Squirrelly the beaver, went on to glory. We bunnies were very sad to lose our adopted brother, Squirrelly, but he had lived a full and active life.

Section II
News of Mayhem and Madness

Now it is time to enter a child-like fantasy world created
by Little Brother and Big Sister.

WARNING!!
*Only those with a colorful imagination that can visualize a world out of the
ordinary may proceed. You've been warned..*

Yak Alert 1!

"It is said that the flying yak has been angered by the death, or alleged murder, of Squirrelly. The flying yak has been spotted flying over the Atlantic Ocean. Those living in Chicago are put on alert of this danger."

-Iamlying Magazine

Editor, Lester the walking Fish

Yak Alert 2!

"The nation has gone berserk. The Flying Yak has frightened many people. While flying over the ocean, he is spreading hate. Fish are losing their minds and attacking people. Here is the story from Eskimo Eji:

"I was sitting on a layer of ice fishing when I felt a fish on my line. As I began to pull the fish in, I noticed there was a hard pull. I got a little closer to the hole cut into the ice. As I looked into the hole, I noticed something flicker and as it got closer, something told me to move. I ducked my head and a spear came flying through the water. I stood on my feet and turned around, and what do you know? Some angry mud puppies lined up for war, barking and saying many hateful things. I was doomed."

"This has been Slyckster Pi Thon for Slanderous News."

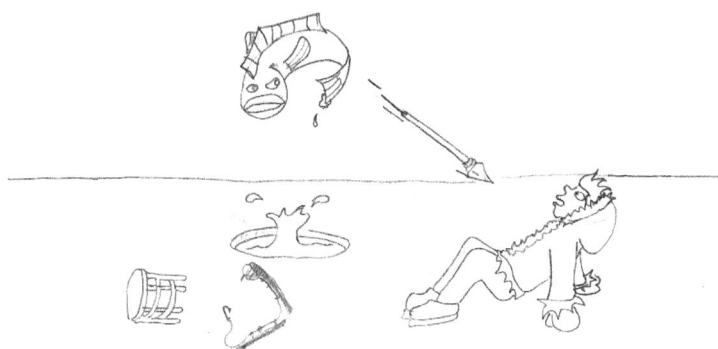

Now it is time for a commercial break…

Have you ever thought about having a facelift?

"Sometimes I sit and wonder, 'What if I had the mouth of an anteater? Would I still like hamburgers? Would I enjoy chewing bubble gum? Would a yawn give me the same satisfaction? What would the dentist tell me?'

Well, we at Faces For Less often think about that, too. What if you had the mouth of an anteater? Would you still have lips? Could you kiss your forehead? Would you have to still shave?

Have you been disgusted with what you see in the mirror every time you look in it? Well, worry no more, because we have the product for you. This new product is guaranteed to remove loose facial skin, teeth, and hair. This new product is called Batter-E-Acid. We can make your dreams a reality! After many years of our surgeons practicing on neighborhood stray dogs, we are confident we can make a totally new you. Give us a call today and begin your journey to a distinct new face that is guaranteed to get the attention of those around you.

The product should be used with the assistance of a trained plastic surgeon, which might not even use the product when performing your surgery. It has been noted that experienced car mechanics work well with our product while working in an auto shop. If you don't like the result, we have a money-back guarantee. Try our free 1 oz sample. Just pay $59.99 for shipping.

Give us a call at 1-888-Fix-ErUp and let us give you a look others will envy."

Before Batter-E-Acid

After Batter-E-Acid

Pink Squirrel News 1!

"Warning! Warning! There is an infected pink squirrel loose. He is very upset and foaming at the mouth. Scientists think that he took a bite out of an acorn, which a little kid touched after playing with his earwax. The squirrel must be sedated and the wax scrapped from his tongue."

Pink Squirrel News 2! Months later

"The authorities have been alerted! Reports are coming in all over the globe about how the Pink Squirrel is infecting a lot of slugs in the warmer climates of Antarctica. It has been brought to our attention that the infected slugs can produce pink mucus, which clearly links it to the Pink Squirrel. The squirrel infected the slugs by kissing its feelers on top of its head. As our brother station mentioned it, this disease is highly contagious to those in warm climates who live in any part of Antarctica, specifically to those without fur. We are feverishly working on a cure for this. All we can hope for, at this point, is that the disease does not spread to the cooler parts of the country, as the Pink Squirrel is an avid flyer.

The child who started all this has not been apprehended due to the fact that the parents are well-known, highly influential people. The child's pediatrician has reluctantly provided copies of the child's health records. In the records, it is noted how the earwax looks very intimidating and it actually melted the examining instruments used for the ears. Pictures were furnished concerning his physical, so the evidence is conclusive that we have the correct child. But again, the parents of this child refuse to have the child's name and identity be told. All we can tell you is that the child goes by the name of Humperdin Snuff and lives in the suburb of Dripville.

That's all.

Wee C. Morebutts reporting for Slanderous News."

Moose Alert!

"Warning: Moose with rabies! Be careful out there. The Moose can be recognized by his antlers. His antlers are growing from his chin and he is missing a tooth. More to come!"

Newt gone mad!

Young Boy was mangled to death when his pet newt turned on him. Young Boy was arrested two weeks prior to this incident for training newts to kill at will. He had his own special newt, which he often fed red-hot Cajun pepper in order to enhance his predator instincts. On the night of the mangling, there was a stare down between the boy and his newt. It is said that the newt gave him the stare of death, but the boy did not take him seriously. The boy tried to intimidate the newt like he usually does, but the newt was very angry. That night he was given a Cajun pepper with a dash of cinnamon. Young Boy came into range of about 6 inches when the newt blinded him by spitting some tobacco in his eye. The boy went into frenzy from not being able to see. The newt leapt on the boy and clawed him to death. The police have not been able to get into the house to arrest the newt because the newt had taken over the house. They say he is not working alone and that the Flying Yak has been seen with him on several occasions.

Brink of War!

"Lin Baden, of the Southern tribe of Keeto, has put an all-out attack against the Blind Pandas of the North. From what we can tell, the Pandas have flown southwest into opposing territory, and unbeknownst to them, right into Keeto territory. Since Lin Baden has not been able to walk after the car ran over his right foot, he has been slow to attack, but vows to attack nonetheless. He came out an aggressive male from the time he hatched. He has always hated the Pandas. Rumor has it that a Panda ate his youngest brother, Zin, after the spreading of hate and thus started this war on Blind Pandas.

These stories and more regarding the ongoing saga of Lin vs. the Pandas of the North will be reported as we receive them.

Signing off,

Red Tree Frog"

War!

Red Tree Frog brings the breaking news once again.

"It is confirmed in conjunction with our brother station that the Flying Yak has been spotted licking the window of Young Boy's home. There is also evidence of the Flying Yak's association with the angry newt.

Finally, it has been brought to our attention that, once again, the southern tribe of Keeto has some involvement in this case. Lin Baden, the Keeto leader, refuses to make comments. That is fine, as we do not have an interpreter available. From reading the salamander's body language, Lin appeared to be saying, 'My brother will be avenged! I am very happy that this has transpired. This has brought the nation to its knees'.

I may not agree with the newt on all aspects, but his message is clear. "If you train us to do what it is we do, we will do." These were strong gestures, coming from such an influential leader.

We now turn to the Northern Pandas, where they have summoned the Skunk Troop to back their efforts. Never before has anyone witnessed such confusion and such chaos amongst a group. Lin Baden and his angry Keeto tribe have gone head-to-head with the group of Blind Pandas. From what our reporters have told us, the Blind Pandas allegedly have the upper hand in the battle.

"They may be blind, but they are big", reports Wee C. Morebutts.

Just when Lin was about to take over and crush the Pandas, the winds changed directions and everyone was stopped in their tracks. We at the network immediately grabbed our gas masks because we remembered the Skunk Troop would be helping in this battle. Before they could get on the war grounds, Lin and his group began to retreat. Once again, he vowed to get revenge for his foot and his late brother. Lin is expecting his first dozen of kids some time this week and will, therefore, not be able to fight with the Pandas until he is finished hatching the eggs".

We have not forgotten that the Pink Squirrel is still on the loose and those of us who are tasty, are put on alert. Given that the young child, Humperdin Snuff, a human who was attacked and infected last week was not as tasty, we who are delicious are frightened for our lives. Although during this battle we have not seen Pinky, we understand that he is in hiding not too far away.

Signing Out,

Red...

Now it is time for another commercial break…

Ground breaking invention

Aren't you tired of running to the washroom three to four times a day? Wouldn't you like to take five Ex-Lax tablets and not have to run to the washroom? There has been a new invention that will revolutionize the world. Try our new NO-GO tablet. Side effects are rare and generally mild. NO-GO contains one special ingredient straight from the motherland. One tablet will last a lifetime, if used correctly. Below are the ingredients and instructions on usage.

Ingredients: Dung Beetle Larvae

After eating a heavy meal, wait 1 hr. Make small incision on tablet with knife or razor and insert tablet into your backend (tablet will not work orally, gastric acids kill Dung Beetles). After inserting the tablet, quickly cork it! Old wine bottle corks work well!

Mild side effects may include:

- Light bleeding every week.

- Tingling sensations that can lead to a burning or ripping sensation.

- If not corked correctly, you will eventually have house pests.

Special announcement:

Happy Birthday!

Peace has rung out between the wild beasts of the earth. The Flying Yak has been seen spreading love for two hours. You could hear the mating calls of the salt-water fish. The newt has been passing ointment to people he has spit on. All this is in remembrance of a special baby that was born on this day.

The ancestors of the Yak had found a baby in the winter among a herd of cattle. It was below zero, but the baby was kept warm from a fresh pile of dung. They noticed the baby because they could see steam coming from the fresh pile of dung and went to gather around and get some heat. Then they saw the precious baby sleeping with a smile on her face. (To this day, we think she was smiling because of the aroma.) They decided to call the baby Ga-Mil-Pew. The name had a meaning among the beasts. The word 'Ga' stands for I. The word 'Mil" means "smell" in the salt-water fish language, and "Pew' means "dung" in the newt language.

Today is the day we all sing, "I smell dung!"

Thank You

We would like to thank our sponsors, No-Go Tablets and Batter-E-Acid Facelifts, for their ongoing support. We were first drawn to these two outstanding companies by their phenomenal acts of service to community. It is because of sponsors such as these that we were able to produce this book.

ABOUT THE AUTHOR

Kevin and Erica grew up on the southwest side of Chicago in a tight-knit family of 7. All the children loved the outdoors and acquired new animals as pets daily. They had different types of pets ranging from lizards and ferrets to fish and birds. They often used their imagination to create fun and laughter, which often spilled out onto their neighborhood. From writing songs and learning martial arts with no formal instruction, to gymnastics and practicing karate on each other, they have certainly come a long way.

Today Kevin has a more tame lifestyle being a husband to Susan Pamon and a father, while working as an Software Engineer. He still has not lost any of his humor from childhood, but has found other methods that are safer to share with those around him.

Erica is a wife to Eddie Johnson and a mother, while finishing her Masters Degree in Education. Her love for children and watching their faces light up while reading was a driving force behind the writing of this book and the ones to come.

Contact us at pamon.johnson@yahoo.com

www.ingramcontent.com/pod-product-compliance
Lightning Source LLC
Chambersburg PA
CBHW071436040426
42445CB00012BA/1380